25 Tough Questions
on the
Catholic Faith

With 25 Expert Answers

Editor
Mgr Keith Barltrop

All booklets are published thanks to the
generous support of the members of the
Catholic Truth Society

CATHOLIC TRUTH SOCIETY
PUBLISHERS TO THE HOLY SEE

Questions

1 Why would a good God allow so much suffering in the world?

Our human sympathy and our sense of fairness can leave us outraged that the world should be filled with so much undeserved suffering. If we are told there is a God who is in charge of our world, then we naturally call into question a being who is in a position to rectify a cosmic injustice and yet appears to do nothing. Religious literature is filled with the voices of those who cry out to God in incomprehension. The Jewish book of Job challenges the Lord and the Hindu Bhagavad Gita challenges Krishna each in their different ways to account for the pain of the world. Jesus on the cross cries out "My God, my God, why have you abandoned me?" And for many, a God who appears to do nothing in the face of such cries might as well not be there.

Mysteriously, though, the encounter with suffering does not always lead to the abandonment of faith in an all-powerful and good God. For many people even the harshest parts of their experience become integrated (not without a struggle) into a relationship with God which is somehow deep enough to bear the paradox of suffering.

We might ask, is it not irrational for a person who has had to endure trauma to continue to believe in a good God? But we find that we are not in a position to decide. Each person copes with their own suffering in the context of a personal affective world, an experience, a set of beliefs and goals over which the philosopher cannot sit in judgment. If someone does not think that life is only worthwhile if it is continuously pain free, the fact that she is enduring a painful illness will not be a reason for her to abandon faith in a good God – though the situation may well challenge her core beliefs. We may question her belief but we are not in a position to say that she is being irrational.

We can however approach the question more abstractly: is it irrational in general to believe in a good God in the face of a world of suffering? Here there are a number of things we need to consider. Are suffering and death (the things we most commonly reproach God for) essentially bad? Can we demonstrate that our world could have been created better, without the unfair suffering which is so clearly an evil for those who endure it?

Is death bad? The ancient philosopher Epicurus urges that we should not fear death, because it is not an event in our lives. It simply belongs to the life cycle whereby some beings cease to exist so that others can come into being. Whether it is the end of conscious existence, as Epicurus believed, or a transition to a new life, as

Christian faith teaches, in neither case is it clear how we can label it, in itself, good or bad.

When we look at suffering, we observe that it is a consequence of our capacity to feel in general. The capacity has evolved to help us cope with and survive in a hard edged world. But is it a bad thing that we feel pain if put our hand into a flame? Is it bad that we feel ill when there is something physically wrong with us? Is it bad that all our actions have physical consequences and that some of these hurt? Again it seems hard to decide whether suffering is good or bad in itself.

Can we show definitively that our world could have existed without unfair suffering? We might imagine a world in every respect like ours, but without tectonic shifts that cause buildings to collapse and people to die painfully, or in which people can never do harm to one another either by accident or by design. Such a world might well have no unfair suffering. But would it still be our world – a world in which we can live and grow and take delight? If we can say 'yes' with certainty, then we can also say that it is irrational to believe that a good God created our world, rather than the imaginary one. But it would be a bold philosopher who claimed such certainty was strictly rational.

Ultimately, Christian faith does not so much attempt to resolve the question of suffering as to transform it. By claiming that in the Incarnation God entered our world of suffering and took it on himself, Christianity places a sacrificial love symbolised by the crucifix in the very centre. Faith tells us that Christ's crucifixion was his greatest moment of glory, because it was "a death he freely accepted" (*Eucharistic Prayer 2*), and that our own suffering can be given infinite value by being united with his in love. Suffering is transformed into sacrifice, one of the most powerful forces in the world.

2 Isn't religion, including Catholicism, divisive and a major cause of wars?

Both history and current events show that religion is certainly one factor in many wars and conflicts, from the Crusades to the troubles in Northern Ireland and the rise of Al Qaeda.

Furthermore, some of the attitudes fostered by religious belief might appear to encourage war and violence. The very establishment and survival of the people of Israel in their own land entailed war against the peoples already there, and an often bloody struggle against these peoples' gods, who were regarded as posing a constant threat to the purity of worship of the one true God. A major theme of Old Testament spirituality is God's power crushing Israel's enemies in battle against overwhelming odds, and the Psalms are full of the violent imagery associated with this.

Jesus himself, though he made it clear that his kingdom was not of this world, and even allowed himself to be captured and put to death, said that he had "not come to bring peace, but a sword" (*Mt* 10:34), and on one occasion used violence to expel the traders from the

Temple (*Mt* 21:12). There are texts in Islam and Hinduism, too, which could be interpreted as justifying warfare in the name of truth. Only Buddhism seems free from this trait, which perhaps helps explain why it, and the New Age spiritualities often associated with it, are popular in a time like ours which is weary of war.

Behind all these religious texts is an understanding that faith gives access to the truth; that this truth is essential for humans to believe if they are to be saved from the evil that is part of the human condition; and that this truth is revealed to a particular people who thus have the mission of guarding it and possibly of spreading it to others.

These attitudes are very difficult for people in our society to accept. Many people today do not believe there is such a thing as 'the truth,' only what is true for you or me. They would not accept the need to be saved by believing something, but consider that we must solve our own problems. Finally, the need for different cultures and beliefs to co-exist in a pluralist world seems to render the idea of a chosen people with a missionary task dangerous.

As a consequence, it is widely felt that anybody who claims to have the truth today is a kind of terrorist. Religion is felt to be acceptable provided it does not take itself too seriously, provided it remains a private affair, and does not attempt to convert others or to enter the sphere of public life. Any other kind of religion is dismissed as fundamentalism. Thus, ironically, any kind of faith which does not conform to Western liberal expectations is increasingly subjected to violence itself.

This reminds us of the other side of the coin, which is that believers themselves have often been violently persecuted in the name of the state. Jews and Christians suffered under the Roman Empire, Moslems and Jews under so-called Christian states, and Christians continue to suffer in various countries today. There is no avoiding the charge that true religion is threatening to worldly power. "All who desire to live a godly life in Christ Jesus will be persecuted." (2 *Tm* 3:12)

However, it is important to distinguish the unchanging beliefs of a religion from elements of human culture which inevitably enter it but change over time. St Paul accepted the institution of slavery, but that does not mean slavery is part of Christian belief: the reverse, in fact, since Christian faith was demonstrably responsible for its eventual abolition.

For the European tribes who accepted Christianity, warfare was something glorious, linked with romance and celebrated in tales of chivalry which gave us some of our greatest literature, art and even music: think of the *1812 Overture*. Our culture is not so comfortable with any celebration of violence, as evidenced by the outlawing of hunting. Yet we realise that war may still be necessary on occasion, and a certain military culture will accompany it.

The Catholic Church is always guided by the Holy Spirit to respond to the challenges of each age. Among those challenges today is how to present Catholic truth confidently while respecting the freedom of others and the value of dialogue with other faiths. Another is how to foster peace among nations with very different cultural and political traditions. Pope John Paul II gave a strong lead in urging against the invasion of Iraq. In this he showed that in the last analysis, it is not religion that is the cause of wars, but the fear that lies in human hearts and which can have as strong an influence in a democratic country as in a totalitarian one.

3 Why does Catholicism produce so much guilt in its followers, especially about sex?

Guilt has had a rough ride in the 20th century, largely because of popular versions of Freudian theory. According to these, guilt is the stick with which the superego beats down and represses natural impulses (themselves morally neutral), thereby causing intolerable pressures in the self which lead to various forms of neurosis. Since the natural impulses discussed have often been sexual ones, sexual guilt is readily identified as a source of neurosis and therefore a Bad Thing. Guilt by association.

Nevertheless, even in Freudian theory, guilt is a universal phenomenon. It is a part of the human condition and can be explored as such. Socio-biologists, interested in the origins of the various emotions underpinning human social behaviour, suggest that guilt together with shame helps regulate behaviours within all human groups in ways that – at least in their evolutionary origins – supported the survival of the group. Guilt is an emotive response to a failure in reciprocity within the group and prompts the guilty party to make amends, while shame is a more ethically ambiguous reaction to loss of status within the group, often entailing loss of self-esteem for the individual, but preserving group hierarchies. On such reasoning religion is not the source of either response.

Clearly, however, any ethical system entails public and private judgments on the quality of actions and of character. These judgments are supposed to make a difference and, by triggering reactions of guilt or shame (or sense of rightness or pride), to alter the behaviour of individuals. Insofar as religions include ethical systems, they too make judgments about what is right or wrong, sinful or virtuous. Thus anyone who commits themselves to such a religion is likely to be exposed to guilt and shame – but because it is ethical, not because it is religious.

Is a sense of guilt a Bad Thing? In actual fact, we expect those who have caused harm to others to feel remorse, shame and guilt and to make amends for what they have done. Those who can feel no such remorse we call psychopaths. Our problems with guilt or shame occur when we see them aroused by things which we regard as ethically acceptable. While our unreflected judgments and emotive responses are often culturally or socially embedded, all of us, religious or not, learn to critique that ethical inheritance on the way to ethical maturity. As a result we can end up disagreeing about what we should feel guilty for. Nevertheless as ethical people we continue to accept that there are some cases where guilt is an appropriate response.

Clearly Catholicism (in common with many traditional cultures) has a conservative set of norms regarding sexual behaviour. One would expect, therefore, a higher incidence of guilt and shame in those who transgress or have difficulty with them than in groups that have less stringent norms. But whether this is a good or bad thing will depend on how you judge the individual norms themselves – which is a matter for ethical debate – not on the fact that people feel guilty about transgressing them. And what applies to sexuality applies to every other area of human life.

In fact Christianity has always recognised pathological forms of guilt and shame as a Bad Thing. It calls them 'scruples' – the constant nagging of old failures and the inability to escape from a sense of personal worthlessness. It understands this as a spiritual malaise which inhibits the journey into Christian freedom. It is an inability to live the fundamental Christian belief that the burden of sin (the guilt, shame, punishment) really is removed, not by our own struggles, but by the gracious gift of God. Indeed many Christian lives have only entered maturity after a profound personal experience of divine forgiveness and freedom from a guilt that overwhelms.

Insofar as Catholicism (like any ethical philosophy) encourages its adherents to reflect on and take responsibility for their actions, it increases the opportunities for awareness of failure, and so for experiencing guilt and shame. Yet because it preaches a Gospel of grace with reconciliation at its heart, in its pastoral care it endeavours to release individuals from the paralysing effects of such failure, liberating them for an ethic of creative goodness, confident of their own (and others') infinite value in the sight of God.

4 How can anyone believe in a religion which accepts Creation when we know that evolution is a sufficient explanation for the world?

The Catholic Church believes that our universe is created and sustained by God. Though it believes this partly on the basis of the Biblical tradition, it does not any more believe (as do some other Christian and Jewish groups) that the account of creation in the book of Genesis is true in a literal sense. As a result the Church accepts the broad modern scientific consensus on the history of the physical universe from the physics of the Big Bang to the account of the development of complex life on earth provided by evolutionary theory. Since neither of these theories has anything specific to say for or against the existence of a creator God, the Church finds no inconsistency in this position.

But even if belief in a creator God is not inconsistent with belief in the science of the origins of the universe, some people may still argue that it is superfluous, in that the belief adds nothing to our explanation of the universe. This is the kind of argument Richard Dawkins presents in the 'Blind Watchmaker,' in which he specifically criticises the naturalist and clergyman William Paley for making an inference from the design-like features present in the biological realm to a designer. There are indeed objects (like the eye) which reveal an intricate organisation of parts to produce a result for the good of the organism. But this is only surprising if we take out of account the vast lengths of evolutionary time which genes have to mutate and be selected in interaction with their environment. The eye only seems an improbable accident if we ignore the tiny incremental steps and the millions of alternative evolutionary pathways that would have led to eye-like objects in the world. The origins of life and consciousness, and the organisation evident in the biological realm can be completely and sufficiently explained in terms of the random mutation of genes and the natural selection of their phenotype expressions. This provides an explanation in the simplest terms without any need to refer to God. A reasonable, scientifically minded person therefore has no reason to believe in a creator/designer God.

This argument is plausible if we assume that the only rational grounds for believing in a creator God are that the belief forms a part of the best scientific explanation of features of the physical world. But this is unlikely ever to be the case, given that physicists, chemists and biologists frame their ultimate explanations in terms of what is repeatable and testable: matter, energy, and laws of nature.

God simply doesn't enter into the equations. In other words the argument is a tautology – it is true by its own definitions. This suggests two considerations: Are there reasons for believing in God which are not to do with providing physical explanations? Can we be sure that a complete physical explanation of things in the world is always sufficient? We take the second of these first.

The objects of the world which are most immediate to us are actually our fellow human beings. Yet it is clear when we try to explain human events, that no physical account on its own is sufficient. Here, the principal regularities which are explanatory, useful and of predictive power, must be expressed in terms of desires, wishes, thoughts intentions and dispositions of the persons involved. But if personal explanations are such an important and useful feature of our immediate world then they already have a legitimate place in the universe. It is, therefore, after all, not unreasonable to suggest, by analogy, that purpose and intention might have a role in the particular physical pathway of our universe from the Big Bang to the emergence of intelligent life, whether directly (interaction) or indirectly (framing the universe's laws).

But in the end, most people do not believe in God because they believe that they need an explanation for the universe. They believe in God because of a quality of experience: an encounter with something powerful, personal and profoundly different. They do not believe in the creator God because they are unable to understand a physical explanation of how things got to be the way they are. Rather they supplement bare physical explanation with reference to a creator God, because they have already encountered that mysterious other, who permeates their whole reality.

5 Why are Catholics so strongly opposed to abortion? What about the right of women to choose?

The Church is against all direct abortion because it involves the ending of innocent human life. The sanctity of life begins at conception when sperm fertilises the egg. From that moment there is a new being with its own DNA, distinct from its parents. Its cells are already multiplying on their own initiative. So a distinct human being, growing naturally into maturity, exists in the womb. There is no dispute about this.

A problem emerges only when we ask whether every human being deserves to be called a person. The Universal Declaration on Human Rights states that personhood extends to human beings from conception until natural death. After the Holocaust people saw the need to protect the dignity of every human being under the mantle of personhood recognising in them absolute and inalienable rights. In recent years, however, there has been a trend to use the idea of personhood to deny rights to certain classes of human beings, including the unborn, the elderly, infants and the terminally ill. History is full of warnings of the danger on denying some human beings their basic human rights.

Beyond legally enshrined human rights, God has revealed that every human being is created in his own image, loved by him from all eternity and predestined for eternal life.

In countries where abortion is legal, virtually all terminations are for social reasons where conception was not through rape or incest, where there is no abnormality in the foetus and there is no danger to the mother's health. Even in these cases we could not regard abortion as a solution. Evidence is growing that many mothers suffer long-term stress when they seek to solve problems by doing away with their unborn child. Often they are haunted by the suspicion that they should have protected their child. But now it is too late. They need a lot of healing to be freed of their sense of guilt and despair.

Some say that abortion is the lesser of two evils and that sometimes you have to do evil so that good may come. But how can killing another human being be a greater good? For whom is it better? Even if the foetus is deformed, what kind of world do we create when we say it is better for some people not to be born?

Those who claim a woman's right to choose say a woman has a right to do what she likes with her own body. But no-one has such a right absolutely. The law places many restrictions on what we can do with our bodies, such as having the right to block public access or to commit suicide. Society frowns on a pregnant woman taking illegal substances that would harm her unborn child. It is just as legitimate to deny her using her body with the effect of killing her child. Many women support the Church's teaching as an affirmation of their feminine dignity.

This teaching is not about choosing the baby's life over its mother's. If we had to kill the mother in order to save her unborn child that would be wrong too. When a pregnant woman has a heart-attack it is permissible to give her anaesthesia and operate on her, even though it is likely that she will spontaneously abort. Similarly when she develops cancer of the uterus it is permissible to remove her womb to save her life, even though the foetus she is carrying will perish as a result. Again, if her pregnancy is ectopic it is ethical to remove her fallopian tubes even if it means the embryo will not survive. In these cases there is no intention to destroy the embryo. The intention is to save the mother and, if anything could have been done to save the child, it would have been.

The Church's teaching says all human life is sacred and all innocent life is protected by her voice.

6 Why is the Catholic Church so negative about gay people?

The Church has a positive understanding of every person, including the homosexual person. Every person without exception is created in the image of God and is predestined for heaven. We are all sacred, loved by God, absolutely valuable to him and have inalienable dignity as his children.

It is because of our dignity as made in the likeness of God that we are called to live good and pure lives. The Bible says we are children of God with a glorious destiny and, to prepare for it, we have to purify ourselves to be more and more like God.

God made us like himself in our souls, bodies and sexuality. The Trinity of Father, Son and Holy Spirit are three persons untied in love. For us to be like him we need to be in personal loving relationships.

This is why God made us male and female. His image is in our whole being. Even our bodies are made to be vessels of his love. Male and female bodies naturally complement each other as a sign that people are made to complete each other by loving as God loves, in life-giving communion. We need each other in order to bring out the image of God in us and to make full sense as a person.

We cannot deny this image of God and his divine Love in our bodies. It would be to say that his Word did not become flesh and that our bodies are just brute facts to do what we like with and not part of God's vision of who we really are.

As sexual beings, our bodies are made for intercourse that expresses the marriage vows. Sexual intercourse outside of this is a contradiction. It creates total flesh union in the absence of union of souls in life-long commitment. It divides the person, body against soul. This lie applies for heterosexual sex and homosexual sex.

Of course there is a difference. Heterosexual couples can marry but homosexual ones cannot. This is because marriage is a Christian testimony about the meaning of our flesh as created for another. Homosexual sex, male or female, sees no sense in the idea that our flesh is made by God as a gift to another. Instead it believes we have a right to make our flesh do what we want it to do, providing it is with another consenting adult. Whether this involves mutual masturbation, oral or anal sex, such acts do not complement the dignity of partners and ultimately do not satisfy our needs to give ourselves as persons. Though they may bring temporary consolation, excitement and pleasure they do not build genuine lasting relationships or foster peace of life and soul. Often they lead to a sense of dejection and despair. On average homosexual partnerships last no more than eighteen months and those that last longer tend not to be monogamous but involve multiple partners. Homosexual sexual patterns are much more promiscuous than heterosexual ones, with all the moral dissolution of life this entails.

The Church hopes that homosexual persons can form sincere, faithful and loving friendships, but if these become genital they cause deadly harm to our faith, our dignity as made in God's image and our development as persons.

It means a painful choice for the homosexual person. He can have homosexual sex with serious negative consequences. Or he can live a celibate life without the consolation of authentic sexual intimacy. St Paul talks of a sadness that leads to death and a sadness that leads to life. The homosexual person is called by God to take up the heavy cross of celibacy but in the consolation that it is a call to authentic love, lived in a life of grace and with a promise of eternal glory.

7 Why should I bother with institutional religion when I can choose my own spiritual path from all that's on offer in different religions and spiritualities?

If salvation in Christ is offered to all men and women, what difference does belonging to the Church make? If we have the autonomy to respond to God's call to holiness or not, have we not the freedom to find holiness outside of the Church? With the myriad expressions of spirituality available in a modern pluralistic society, such questions are more than rhetorical. "Some say that the Christian religion is patriarchal and authoritarian, that political institutions are unable to improve the world... The fact that what were once central elements in society are now perceived as untrustworthy or lacking in genuine authority has created a climate where people look inwards, into themselves, for meaning and strength" (*Jesus Christ: Bearer of the Water of Life*). The Second Vatican Council teaches that we have the right and the duty to seek truth. In a culture that celebrates self and diverse expressions of spirituality are we capable of finding truth?

Contemporary western culture inclines towards self reliance rather than belonging to the Church; yet as spiritual beings created in relationship to God and to one another, the answers we can find by looking inwards are necessarily limited. In his book *The Idea of the Holy*, Rudolf Otto maintains that religion cannot work on a level of rational self-exploration. The relationship of the human person to God is as ineffable as the divine itself, and cannot be seen as simply 'morality touched with emotion'. To Otto, this indescribable and irrational need to relate to the divine is not only characteristic of a few individuals, but of society as a whole. In the same way, the Second Vatican Council teaches, 'it has pleased God to call human beings together to share his life not merely as individuals without relation to each other but to make of them a people in which his children who are scattered far and wide may be brought together into one' (*Ad Gentes 2*). Our common humanity unites us in a common search for God.

In the same way, Paul Heelas and Linda Woodhead distinguish religion from spirituality in their introduction to *The Spiritual Revolution – Why Religion is Giving Way to Spirituality*. Religion subordinates spirituality as 'subjective life' to a higher authority of transcendent meaning, goodness and truth. Religion is not separate from spirituality; rather it provides the necessary traditions, rationalisation, and authority for a spiritual way of living.

Pope John Paul II's Apostolic Letter *Novo Millennio Ineunte* addressed the great interest in spirituality found in the secular world of today. While acknowledging the ways in which this desire for spiritual expression was being met, it both affirmed and challenged the Church: "But we who have received the grace of believing in Christ, the revealer of the Father and the Saviour of the world, have a duty to show to what depths the relationship with Christ can lead."

In the same way, Pope Benedict XVI warns against a cafeteria approach to religion, or a self-obsessed way of living that leads to a selective adaptation of moral and ethical values that is subjective. Rather than being a challenge to institutional religion, turning inwards isolates human beings and can lead to an obsession with self, its values and capacities. While the Church is a mystery, we believe that God calls his people to be one. We are a community, and the living body of Christ. God entrusts his word to the Church, that she might interpret, teach and defend the revelation of salvation to every generation and every people.

8 Doesn't the toleration and cover-up of so much sex abuse show that the Catholic Church is hypocritical?

Since the 1960s there has been an increasing awareness within our society as a whole about the existence and impact of sexual abuse. Local authorities began developing procedures for managing allegations of abuse in the late 60s and early 70s.

As our awareness increased it became a sad reality that no organisation working with children was immune to the horrors of child sexual abuse occurring within that organisation. This regrettably was also true of the Catholic Church.

The Church has dealt with this problem in various ways around the world. In England and Wales, the Catholic Church invited Lord Nolan in 2000 to carry out a review and set out a framework for best practice and prevention in child protection. His report *A Programme for Action*, 2001, did that and established the Catholic Office for the Protection of Children & Vulnerable Adults (COPCA). As well as the national office, COPCA has worked with Bishops and Leaders of Religious Orders to establish independently chaired Child Protection Commissions within every Diocese and Religious Congregation to implement child protection procedures.

These arrangements have recently been reviewed by an independent group, the Cumberlege Commission, whose full report is available at: *www.cumberlegecomission.org.uk.*

Among its conclusions were the following: "A great deal has been achieved in a remarkably short time to raise the profile of child protection on local agendas. It is clear COPCA's achievements have been considerable…making a huge contribution to strengthening the Church's capacity to keep children safe. As a result the Church has been able to demonstrate a new professionalism and greater transparency and accountability in the way it deals with child protection issues, now justly recognised by the statutory authorities."

The Catholic Church of England and Wales is unique amongst faith groups in Britain in publishing Annual Reports since 2002, detailing all allegations of abuse and how they were managed. The most recent report, 2007, is available on: *www.csas.uk.net.*

9 I have heard that exorcisms are frequently performed in the Catholic Church. How can you believe in that?

Christ performed exorcisms himself (see, for example, *Mk* 1:34), and instructed his Church to perform them (e.g. *Mk* 3:15; 16:17). In obedience, the Church has carried out exorcisms from the beginning and will continue to do so till the end. So this question could be answered with the words of Jesus himself: "Is not this where you go wrong, that you know neither the Scriptures nor the power of God?" (*Mk* 12:24)

If angels and spirits, good or bad, exist, why is everyone not aware of them? They can be perceived directly, not by our five senses, but sometimes by a kind of sixth or 'psychic' sense, which some have more than others. This, however, is always unreliable and God has forbidden us to develop it (*Dt* 18:9-14). He has told us, rather, to rely on his word and on the Holy Spirit, whom he gives to the children of faith. "We have received not the spirit of the world but the Spirit from God that we might understand the gifts bestowed on us by God... The unspiritual (natural or psychic) man does not receive the gifts of the Spirit of God." (1 *Co* 2:12, 14)

When the seventy-two disciples rejoiced that the demons were subject to them, Jesus prayed: "I thank you, Father, Lord of heaven and earth, that you have hidden these things from the wise and understanding and revealed them to babes" (*Lk* 10:21). Salvation begins with the realisation that Our Lord is wiser than we are.

It might be objected that in performing exorcisms, Christ was simply accepting the outlook of his time. However, widely different views were in fact current at the time of Christ. The Sadducees, for example, "say that there is no resurrection or angel or spirit; but the Pharisees acknowledge them all" (*Ac* 23:8). Far from adopting the ideas of the world, Jesus is the light who reveals spiritual reality to the world (*Jn* 1:5; 3:19; 8:12; 9:5). For most of the Old Testament the Devil is more or less hidden; in the New Testament Christ forces him to reveal himself.

Some people believe that the Gospels contain much that the Church later came to believe about Christ rather than what he was really like. However, the Second Vatican Council reminds us (*Dei Verbum* 19) that "Holy Mother Church has firmly and with absolute constancy maintained and continues to maintain that the four Gospels…, whose historicity she unhesitatingly affirms, faithfully hand on what Jesus, the Son of God, while he lived among men, really did and taught for their eternal salvation, until the day he was taken up."

Our faith is in the Incarnation: if we cannot know the Son as he was in his life on this earth, the purpose of his becoming man would be defeated, for we could not have a personal relationship with him through his humanity.

One objection to exorcisms is that people may blame the Devil instead of themselves, and thus evade responsibility and remain very immature. There are many possible wrong turnings and certainly this is one of them, but there is no excuse for it in the teaching of Christ. Read, for example, the Sermon on the Mount (*Mt* 5-7). Neither divine grace nor demonic temptation removes the awe-inspiring dignity of our free will.

How can exorcism be relevant to a society such as ours which does not think in terms of spirits? Spiritual reality is not altered according to the terms in which we choose to think. There is, in fact, a great and growing need of exorcisms. The primary cause is the apostasy of a large part of Europe and the return of the "seven more evil spirits" (*Mt* 12:43-45). The 'New Age' is only one of them. Atheistic materialism is devouring the fruit of the tree of knowledge (*Gn* 2-3) more shamelessly and suicidally than ever before in history. Scientific advances are exploited to commercialise, mechanise, trivialise and dehumanise us. No longer do most people have some sort of innate sense of the natural law. Adultery, contraception, IVF, the vivisection of embryos and the rest all pass as normal. As a society we are throwing away our spiritual and our natural defences at the same time.

How is our unbelieving age to find faith in Christ? As ever, there is a high road and a low road. The high road is to seek the truth, for then the Spirit of truth will guide us from within. The low road is that of sin and suffering and mercy. Along that hard road, exorcism is sometimes a friend in need.

10 Why is the Catholic Church's position on birth control so unreasonable?

The Catholic teaching on artificial contraception arises out of the distinctive belief, rooted in the Jewish-Christian tradition, that man and woman, as images of the creator God, are called to have children, and that all life processes are in God's hands. We can begin exploring this teaching and its effects with the Second Vatican Council's discussion of the significance of family life.

The Council repeated the traditional understanding, that the primary purpose of marriage was to have children, but balanced this by affirming the essential goodness of the sexual union of Christian married couples as a value in itself. The whole of their married life is a sign of the love between Christ and his Church. Their duty to have children reflects their calling to mirror the creative work of God. The Council praised couples who generously choose to have large families, but recognised that families can face hard economic choices and couples may legitimately want to restrict the number of their children. It was left to Pope Paul VI,

with the help of a partly lay commission, to decide
whether the existing teaching on contraception could be
adapted in response.

When Paul came to writing his judgment in *Humanae
Vitae* (1968) he deepened Vatican II's rich vision of
married love and at the same time reiterated the Church's
traditional teaching that the use of artificial contraception
is essentially unworthy – diminishing the sign value of
marriage and interfering with a process that should
always remain ultimately in the hands of God. Natural
family planning was allowed, because this, he argued, left
open the possibility of God's action in a way that artificial
means did not.

As is well-known, reactions to *Humanae Vitae* varied
hugely. Some found the Pope's text inspirational and the
teaching enriched their married life. Some who had been
expecting a change of teaching were hurt by the ruling
and left the Church, while others simply ignored it. It
quickly became an issue not just of ethical truth but of
papal authority.

Pope John Paul II set himself to reaffirm the
instruction in his reflections on the meaning of Christian
married life, which were rooted in biblical text interpreted
through a theology of the embodied person: the *Theology
of the Body*. He argued that artificial contraception is
wrong, not so much because it violates a law of biological
nature, but because it implies a self-contradiction in the

personal expression of love between two people. Sexual union is an act of mutual self-gift freely undertaken by two human persons and expressed through their bodies, which ought to mirror their primordial relationship (communion) with the God of generous and creative love. So to prevent, artificially, the conception of a new life contradicts the very meaning of that act.

More and more people have come to find this catechesis illuminating, and are attracted to a model of married life that is attentive to and respectful of the rhythms of their partner's body. Many still struggle with the Church's teaching and some continue to ignore it. Meanwhile, there is increasing awareness that the contraceptive mentality, against which Pope Paul so courageously took his stand, is intimately bound up with our society's illusion of sexual freedom, which looks enticing but causes immense harm in the form of family breakdown and general loss of self-discipline. The Church is always understanding and patient with those who struggle both morally and intellectually to accept this hard teaching, but each passing year increases the sense that *Humanae Vitae* was prophetic and that ignoring it or ridiculing it is like laughing at a lighthouse on a stormy sea.

11 Why are so many Catholic beliefs based on their own tradition rather than the Bible?

In any discussion on the relationship between the Bible and subsequent tradition it is important to remember two things. The first is that the texts of the Old and New Testaments were written from within pre-existing Jewish and Christian communities. The second is that the choice of which writings were to become the official New and Old Testaments was made by the leaders of pre-existing communities. Thus, for example, the earliest Christian text we have in the New Testament is probably Paul's first letter to the Thessalonians, but Christian communities had already been around for twenty years before he put pen to paper. His letter (and his later writings) were eagerly read around the Christian world for a century before Christian leaders decided that they were core texts reflecting authentic Christianity, and made them part of the canon of the New Testament.

A single text does not tell us everything that is going on in a community at the time of its writing, and however precious that text becomes for later generations of the community, it does not capture every aspect of the real life of the community either at the time of writing or at the time of reading. To take just a few examples, the New Testament canon chosen in the late 2nd century tells us very little about the variety of ways in which Christians actually worshipped in those years. Nor do the descriptions of Church offices in the New Testament letter writers tell us about how the Church system had developed through trials, persecutions and internal disputes up until the 4th century – we need other sources for that.

More controversially, the New Testament texts on their own do not necessarily commit us to reading the classic doctrines of the Trinity and of the two natures of Christ established between the Councils of Nicaea (325) and Chalcedon (451), which is why Jehovah's witnesses can use the Bible in as good faith as orthodox Christians. Church teaching develops in response to awkward questions and each generation's questions are different. For Paul's generation a key issue was, how much of Jewish practice does Christianity have to maintain to be authentic? For the generation of Chalcedon it was, how can we affirm the divinity and the humanity of Christ coherently?

The Christian community, in which the Holy Spirit is ever-present, has a right and a duty to express its faith anew in interaction with the different environments and cultures into which it moves. In the Catholic and

Orthodox traditions any such expression will typically be justified by reference first to a word of scripture, second by reference to official pronouncements (of Church Councils or Church authorities) and third by reference to respected teachers, especially those from the distant past. In this the Christian tradition mirrors some aspects of the Rabbinic Jewish tradition, which, in the Mishnah and the Talmud preserves an account of the different ways that different Rabbis have interpreted the Torah, and uses these as a basis for contemporary debate.

A consequence of this is that practices and beliefs emerge in Catholic and Orthodox Christianity in the course of time which appear very different to what is found in the New Testament. However it is rare to find a practice or belief which cannot be traced back to an awkward question which had to be dealt with, and which does not leave a trail of sentences going back to ancient interpretations of scripture. Thus even a doctrine like the Immaculate Conception of Mary, which can seem especially unwarranted to Protestant Christians, can be traced back to Christian writers of the 4th century who were struggling to make sense of how the humanity of Christ, derived from Mary, could be – as scripture says – without sin.

So why does the Catholic Church have beliefs based on traditions that run alongside the Bible? Most simply, because it is a living community that has evolved through two thousand years and many cultures. Scripture has a vital place in this process and especially the New Testament, as the gift which the ancient Christian communities gave to future generations. But for all Christians, whether Orthodox, Catholic or Protestant, all scripture is interpreted in the light of a tradition confronted with the challenges of the age.

12 Why do Catholics worship Mary and the saints instead of giving all honour to Jesus?

The short answer to this common question is: "We most definitely don't worship Mary and the saints." Catholics worship only God. Mary and the saints are human beings, like ourselves. Indeed, their holiness means precisely that they are more fully human than the rest of us. The sanctity of the saints consists in their loving God and their fellow human beings to a remarkable and, as it is often said, 'heroic' degree. The sanctity of Mary is, Catholics believe, unique among all the members of the human race.

It is true that devotion to Mary has taken forms at certain times and in certain places that have created the impression that she is more than human and the object of worship rather than devotion and reverence. But Mary's unique place in the lives of Catholics is as a member of the Church, one of the faithful. She is a human being, indeed she is the most fully human member of the Church, unique in her faithful response to God and thus unique in holiness. All that is taught by

the Catholic Church about Mary arises from her
relationship with Jesus, and the Catholic understanding
of her role emerges alongside our understanding of
Christ, her son.

The earliest and most important teaching about Mary
is that, as the mother of Jesus, she is the Mother of God.
It is primarily, in other words, a doctrine about Christ,
and only secondarily about his mother. This is the
background to the two doctrines concerning Mary that,
along with her perpetual virginity, have been
controversial outside the Catholic Church, among both
Protestant Christians and non-Christians: namely the
Immaculate Conception promulgated in 1854 and the
Assumption promulgated in 1950.

The dogma of the Immaculate Conception, which,
though promulgated only in the 19th century, goes back
to the earliest centuries of the Church, teaches that Mary
"was, from the first moment of her conception, by the
singular grace and privilege of almighty God and in view
of the merits of Jesus Christ the Saviour of the human
race, preserved free from all stain of original sin." Mary,
according to this teaching, was untouched, uniquely, by
original sin. In practice, this means that she lived in
perfect communion with God from the first instant of her
existence. The reign of sin, in other words, came to an
end in her and the ultimate destiny of us all is realised in
the life of Mary, 'full of grace'.

As Mary's coming into this world was exceptional so, for the same reasons, was her going from this world to the next. Though the doctrine of Mary's Assumption was promulgated only in 1950 by Pius XII, belief that Mary was taken body and soul into heaven first appeared in the 6th century. The view that Mary's body did not corrupt in the grave but was immediately reunited with her soul was common from around the beginning of the 5th century and belief in the bodily assumption of Mary has been held by Christians in both the Western and the Eastern Church ever since. In Eastern Christianity, it is known as the Dormition, the Falling Asleep of the Blessed Virgin Mary.

The doctrine teaches that, by the grace of God and through the redeeming work of her Son, Mary shares already in the fullness of his resurrection. An important corollary of this teaching is that the whole person is saved and redeemed, thus countering falsely spiritual views of human nature, in which the emphasis is placed on the soul at the expense of the body. Human beings are body and soul. But the central significance of the Assumption, as with all doctrines concerning Mary, is its relationship to the saving action of Christ in restoring humanity to the fullness for which we have been created.

Mary's holiness is unique, as is her place in the Church. We pray to her and ask for her prayers. But there are other members of the Church, the saints, who have lived lives of extraordinary holiness, who have loved God and their fellow human beings heroically. We pray to them, also, and ask their prayers. St Paul referred to all members of the Church as 'the saints'. By this, he meant that by our baptism, we all share in the holiness of Christ himself. But some men and women have lived out the grace of their baptism so fully and conspicuously that the Church holds them before us as examples of virtue and holiness to be imitated. These are the canonised saints of the Catholic Church. Saintliness, of course, is not confined to them alone. We all know people whose lives are or have been saintly. But the canonised saints are those about whose holiness there is no doubt and, for that reason, they hold a special place in the lives of Catholics.

13 Where does Catholic belief in Purgatory come from when it isn't mentioned in the Bible? Why do we need to pray for dead people?

We need to remember that for the first generation of Christians nothing that they believed about the afterlife came from the New Testament, because this had not been written, and some of what they did believe would have been influenced by narratives from Jewish writings which never made it into the canon of the Old Testament. Indeed most of the Old Testament writings date from at least four hundred years before the time of Jesus and in those writings there is comparatively little interest in the afterlife: sin and its punishment are dealt with in this world and salvation is worked out in the history of God's people.

Yet by the time of Jesus the afterlife is a hot topic of debate (see *Mk* 12, 18ff, *Ac* 22). The Jewish author Josephus, who was from an aristocratic Jerusalem family of the 1st century AD, describes the belief of the Pharisees in the resurrection of the body at the end of time. Visionary writings from the 2nd Century BC (of uncertain authorship) like the *Book of Enoch* include descriptions of the cave in the heavenly realm where the souls are preserved until that Day. The Qumran writings found in caves by the Dead Sea also speak of the 'visitation' when the righteous shall have everlasting blessing, eternal life, joy without end, while the evil will be destroyed by demons after ages of misery. We catch hints of similar narrative in Daniel 12 (written in the 2nd century during the time of persecution by the Greeks) as well as in Wisdom of Solomon (written in Greek in the 1st century BC). Sin and judgment are now reserved to the end of time, and reward and punishment are for eternity.

A common thread is that there is an in-between-time from the moment of earthly death to the final judgment of the world, when the souls are in a sort of suspension. It is this that makes sense of the account in 2 Maccabees 12 (2nd/1st century BC) where the leader of the Jewish rebellion, Judas, finding idolatrous charms on the bodies of his fallen soldiers, makes sin offerings for them, so that they may be spared on the day of judgment. They still have time.

But time is precisely the issue in the earliest Christian teaching on the afterlife. Jesus was supposed to return and judge the world quickly. Thus there can be no in-between-time. In order to be saved from the wrath, you have to repent and be baptised in the name of Jesus. The working assumption is that though you may have to work hard, you will at least not have to work long before the end time comes. It became clear, though, within half a generation, as Christians started dying, that they were going to have to start coping with a long game. This is precisely one of the main themes of Paul's first letter, written to the Thessalonians. And one of the problems raised by the long game is personal failure of the baptised.

It is left to later generations of Christians to spell out beliefs that are already emerging in a liturgy which, as with Judas Maccabee, prays for the dead. Theologians build on ambiguous references in the New Testament, which refer to 'purifying fire' (1 *P* 1:7, 1 *Co* 3:15) and 'the souls in prison' (1 *P* 3:19). So, for instance Augustine (5th century) speaks of a time of purgation for the spirits of those who have lived neither so badly as to deserve damnation nor so well that they need no mercy and says that they can be helped by the prayers of the saints. Gregory the Great (6th century) deduces from the words of Jesus 'anyone who blasphemes against the Holy Spirit will not be forgiven in this world or the next' that there are some people who can be forgiven in the next world. By the time of Dante, in the Middle Ages, the iconography of the afterlife (including purgatory) is heavily influenced by classical models (Plato's *Republic X* and Virgil's *Aeneid VI*), but the doctrine has grown out of Jewish soil to answer an urgent existential question that was not an issue for the first Christians: what happens if I die and I'm not ready to meet my judge?

14 Why do Catholics confess their sins to a priest? Why not go directly to God?

As Catholics we daily confess our sins directly to God. When we go to bed we examine our conscience and confess our sins to him and he hears and forgives them. Every time we go to Mass we begin with the penitential rite in which we confess our sins to God who has mercy on us, pardons us and takes our sins away. Usually we say the *Confiteor* and confess to Almighty God and to our brothers and sisters. At the end we ask Our Lady, the Angels and Saints and our brothers and sisters to pray to God for our forgiveness.

Going to confession is not a substitute for this kind of confession but complements it. First of all the sacrament has its own unique grace. This grace comes in the form of guaranteed forgiveness, help to understand our sin, sense of sorrow and strength to amend our ways.

Confessing our sins to the priest, who represents both God and our brother and sisters, adds to our understanding of sin and forgiveness in two ways. Representing humanity the priest reminds us that our sin has usually harmed some other person. We should really confess it to every person who was hurt by it. That is not always easy or possible. Confessing to the priest is a sign that we accept that our sin damaged not just God or ourselves but humanity and that we need forgiveness from other people too. But representing God, the priest reminds us that only He can take away our sins. As Jesus said, "Who can forgive sins but God alone?" Jesus gave priests this power when he said, "Receive the Holy Spirit. For those whose sins you shall forgive they are forgiven."

Jesus was talking about serious sin, sometimes called mortal, because it can so fundamentally contradict our relationship with God as to sever it. In our human relationships some offences just need a simple, 'I'm sorry', while others are so damaging that we need to take time out to apologise formally and make amends. Serious offences against the Ten Commandments as taught by the Church need this kind of reconciliation with God in the Sacrament to remove the danger of losing God's grace and salvation. We should not go to Holy Communion until it is forgiven in confession. If we do not have such sins we should always go to Communion because it is a medicine and strengthening for our ordinary Christian life.

Even if we have no serious sins we must go to Confession at least once a year and around Easter time as a reminder that we have damaged the Church by our sins. Of course the Church strongly recommends regular confession, for example monthly. This is not really about reconciliation because our relationship with God is not broken. It is an unsurpassed way of growing in spiritual perfection. It is difficult to grow in holiness without the practice of regular confession.

So do not be put off by the usual obstacles. It does not matter if it is the same sins all the time. We would not want any new sins, would we? Having forgiveness for the same sins is like having the dressing changed on a bad burn. For a while there seems to be no difference but the regular cleansing of the wound brings an eventual healing. Most people usually have some fear of the sacrament. It is much healthier to fear sin than God's mercy. When we sin we should run to confession for forgiveness, help and reassurance from God and the priest.

The only difficulty is the kind of sin the priest cannot forgive when, for example, a person is living in a sexual relationship outside of marriage. Forgiveness needs the intention not to sin again which is impossible when going straight back to a sinful situation. That is why it is so vital to resist the temptation to move in with a partner.

Jesus did not give his priests this power in order to make things difficult for us but to make reconciliation with him easier. The best way to thank him is to use this gift well.

15 How can Catholics believe the Pope is infallible when popes have clearly made mistakes, such as - the Crusades, condemning Galileo and the *silence* of Pius XII?

Catholics believe that the Pope is infallible when he speaks *ex cathedra*, that is 'when in discharge of the office of Pastor of all Christians, by virtue of his supreme apostolic authority, he defines a doctrine regarding Faith and Morals to be held by the Universal Church' (*Vatican I*). An example of this infallibility was the solemn definition of the Assumption of the Blessed Virgin Mary by Pius XII in 1950. Infallibility doesn't mean that the Pope is impeccable (sinless) in his conduct, but that he is protected by the Holy Spirit from error when teaching as the Church's supreme pastor.

Despite possessing the charism of infallibility, the Pope normally uses his ordinary teaching authority when writing Encyclicals or making addresses. This ordinary authority is authoritative rather than infallible and should be respected and followed, although it does not bind us in the same way as an infallible teaching.

When it comes to a Pope's theological opinions or his governance of the Church, it is quite possible for mistakes to be made. Indeed, St Peter himself was criticised by St Paul for his support of Jewish practices in the early Christian community (cf. *Ga* 2:11-16; *Ac* 10:9-11:18).

Critics of infallibility sometimes bring up a number of historical cases that seemingly prove the fallibility and even the heresy of individual Popes. The 7th-century Pope, Honorius I (625-638), is often mentioned because after his death he was actually condemned for his theological views by one of the General Councils of the Church, the third Council of Constantinople (680-681). He was accused of monothelitism, a heresy stating that Christ had one Divine Will, into which was absorbed his Human Will, rather than having a Divine and a Human Will. In effect, the monothelites denied Christ's true humanity. In an attempt to restore peace to the Church, the Pope wrote in a private letter to both a leading Monothelite and a champion of orthodoxy that 'there is but one Will in Christ.' It may be that Honorius, in the words of Leo II, was negligent 'in extinguishing the rising flame of heresy' but in his letters the Pope was not speaking *ex cathedra* and his words can, in fact, be interpreted in an orthodox sense (that there is a unity in Christ and his Wills are not conflicting).

Modern writers often criticise the Papacy's support for the Crusades, its condemnation of Galileo and Pius XII's apparent silence in the face of the Holocaust. Such criticisms tend to simplify the complex historical forces involved and overlook the circumstances of the times. However, none of these examples involve the Pope's infallible teaching authority.

The Crusades were a complex phenomenon, stretching over several centuries and aiming to defend Christendom or recover Christian lands. It is true that a major characteristic of these 'armed pilgrimages' were their authorisation by the Pope himself, who identified the purpose of a particular campaign and granted privileges and indulgences. Indeed the First Crusade originated with the appeal of Pope Urban II at the Council of Clermont (1095). It should be remembered, though, that the Popes often criticised the excesses of crusaders, condemning the anti-Semitic violence that marred the First Crusade and excommunicating all those who sacked Constantinople in the Fourth Crusade. Nor did papal support for the crusades involve the Pope's infallible teaching authority.

In the case of Galileo, it is true that the scientist was condemned for his heliocentric theories by the Congregations of the Holy Office and the Index (not directly by the Pope himself). Galileo's theories were radical for the time and disputed by the majority of scientists, both Catholic and Protestant. The Church was a great patron of the sciences and it is only because Galileo proposed his theories with such imprudence (as a certainty rather than a proposition) and because he tried to apply his discoveries to Sacred Scripture that the Church became suspicious and examined his works. Galileo's views were later universally accepted but his condemnation was a disciplinary matter and did not involve the extraordinary infallible teaching authority of the Pope.

Finally, Pius XII has been widely criticised for his apparent 'silence' concerning the Holocaust. Officially he maintained the Papacy's neutral position and feared that any condemnation of the Nazi regime would worsen the situation for both Jews and Catholics and endanger the security of the Church. However, Pius XII frequently attacked wartime atrocities in his speeches, so that at Christmas 1941 the New York Times called him 'a lonely voice in the silence and darkness enveloping Europe.' He did much to shelter Jews and other refugees in the Vatican and church property throughout Rome. It is clear that Hitler saw the Pope as a great threat rather than a sympathetic ally and there is evidence that the Führer considered kidnapping him. Once again, the Pope's actions should be read in the context of the actual historical situation and the pressures surrounding him, and do not concern his infallible teaching authority. Even if Pius XII could be criticised for not doing more, much of what he did was praiseworthy.

16 Isn't transubstantiation an outmoded doctrine? Isn't it clear that Jesus was speaking symbolically when he told us to eat his body and drink his blood?

The Mass or the Eucharist is regarded by Catholics, Orthodox Christians and by many Anglicans as the greatest of the sacraments, precisely because in this sacrament, the presence of Christ, which is, of course, central to all the sacraments, is made most explicit.

The presence of Christ in the Eucharist is spoken of in Catholic teaching as the Real Presence. 'Real' here does not mean 'authentic' but comes from the Latin *in re*, in the thing itself, namely, the species of bread and wine. And, traditionally, the word 'transubstantiation' has been used to describe the nature of the change that takes place during the Mass through which Christ becomes present under the form of bread and wine.

But belief in the real presence of Christ is nothing new: it is part of the Apostolic Tradition. It is important to remember that controversies concerning how this presence of Christ in the Eucharist is to be understood come only relatively late: there are no such controversies in the early church. Some Protestants claim that the teaching of the Church about the Real Presence was a novel departure from the earliest teaching of the Apostolic Church. But listen to these unequivocal and authoritative voices from the earliest period of the Church's life. St Cyril of Jerusalem (315-87) says: What seems bread is not bread, even if it seems such to the taste, but the body of Christ, and what seems wine is not wine, even though it has its taste, but the blood of Christ. (*Catecheses* 4, 9)

And the great St Ambrose (c 333-397): Perhaps you say: Mine is ordinary bread. But the bread is bread before the words of the sacrament; when the sacrament is added, what is bread becomes the flesh of Christ. (*De Sacramentis*)

The notion of 'transubstantiation' was first used officially to articulate the mode of Christ's presence in the Eucharist in the 13th century at the Fourth Lateran Council in 1215; but it had been used in earlier debates to express what the Church believed about the eucharistic presence. Later, the Council of Trent in the 16th century says that this is simply a most appropriate (*aptissime*) way of talking about the Eucharist. Compare this with what the Thirty Nine Articles have to say about the same way of talking: they forbid it as "repugnant to the plain words of Scripture".

But whatever term is used to express our belief in Christ's presence in the Eucharist, the teaching of the

Catholic Church is clear: what is received under the outward forms of bread and wine, is the whole Christ. The outward forms of bread and wine symbolise, of course, nourishment. But it is Christ, the bread from heaven, who is this nourishment, not bread and wine. And it is communion with the whole Christ that is effected by receiving the consecrated elements. This is a work of grace, not a mechanical transaction, and there is no inward communion with Christ and no increase of grace, without the appropriate dispositions, principally the desire for such communion and the belief that this is truly Christ. But, crucially, the objective presence of Christ in the Eucharist does not depend on the belief of the person receiving communion.

In the early days of the Church, misunderstandings of the Eucharist among pagans abounded. The charge of cannibalism, for instance, was levelled at Christians. But this is a telling criticism, arising from an understandable misapprehension of what was heard to be taking place.

Catholics believe that in the sacrament of the Eucharist, such a change takes place that the reality of the bread gives way to the reality of Christ. Christ is not physically present in the same way that other people are physically present: but he is personally present. So, for instance, when the host is broken, Christ is not broken. When we eat the host, we receive Christ, but Christ is not chewed or broken down by our digestive juices. Indeed,

Christ does not cease to be in heaven when he is made present at the Eucharist.

How this can be is clearly beyond our understanding; just as it is clearly beyond our understanding how Christ can be both man and God. In this sense, even talk of 'transubstantiation' is, itself, inadequate, even if 'most fitting'.

Before the consecration at Mass, the appearances of bread and wine were there because the substance of bread and wine were there. After the consecration, it is the reverse: Christ is sacramentally present because what were the appearances of bread and wine are now sacramental signs of his presence. After the consecration, the body of Christ is sacramentally present just as long as the signs are there.

What happens when we consecrate the bread and wine at Mass is that the body and blood of Christ become present as our food and drink to constitute our sharing in the coming banquet of heaven. This happens not by any change in Christ himself but by a miracle comparable to creation, in which the whole existence of our bread and wine become the existence of Christ. The bread and wine which was present naturally is converted, not by any substantial change, but by the creative power of God, into the body and Christ, which is present not naturally but sacramentally.

17 Why don't Catholics offer Holy Communion to members of other Churches?

Only practising Catholics who are not in a state of serious sin can go to Holy Communion. Christians from other denominations are welcome at the celebration of Mass but not normally to receive the Sacrament.

Other Christian denominations who have Eucharistic services or services of Holy Communion now generally invite everyone to participate. For them the Eucharist is a sign of hospitality. They say that if you invite a friend to your home you invite him to share your table. In this vision restricting Holy Communion to members of the denomination is inhospitable and unchristian.

Catholics do not see the Eucharist from the point of view of hospitality. For us the Eucharist is the most intimate expression of belonging to Christ in the Church. For Catholics a better analogy would be the bridal suite. Just as the marital act is the complete bodily expression of the wedding vow so Holy Communion is the most intimate bodily expression of belonging to the Church. It is reserved for the avowed members and is not shared by others.

For Catholics Holy Communion is an expression of our communion with the Church. This means belonging to the Church through baptism and believing in all that it is and professes to be. It means affirming all that we do at Mass, including the Creed, our union with the Pope and bishops throughout the world, and our communion with the angels and saints in heaven. Those who profess only some of these truths are like people who want to be friends with each other but not married. They may share much of life in common but not complete bodily communion.

The Orthodox Churches are our closest brothers and sisters. With us they trace their priestly origins to the apostles and their priests celebrate valid Masses. The Eucharist common to all of us is identical. We can say of the Eucharist in all these Churches that 'It is the Lord'. In cases where it is impossible to go to our own churches we can, with their permission, receive Holy Communion in these places of worship and they in ours. Until we are fully united, however, we ordinarily do not do so in order to recognise the truth of our brokenness and humbly ask the Holy Spirit to heal our divisions.

There is much more uncertainty about other Christian communities. Since Anglicans do not trace their priestly origins to the apostles there is a substantial question over the validity of their Eucharistic celebrations. It is not possible for Catholics to hold of Anglican Eucharist that it is the Lord in the same way. Out of reverence for the

Real Presence of Christ in the Eucharist we should not act
as though he is present when this is not warranted.

Protestant Churches do not usually make a claim that
Jesus is really present in the Eucharist in the way
Catholics believe. They do not believe in the ministerial
priesthood or in the Holy Sacrifice of the Mass. Although
we share their belief that Jesus is the Lord and pray and
work with them in a spirit of fraternity and charity,
sharing communion with them would entail too
substantial a denial of our own understanding of the faith.
(However, the local bishop may give permission for a
non-Catholic who shares our faith in the Real Presence
and who cannot go to a Eucharist of their own church, to
receive communion with us on a specific occasion if there
would be a genuine spiritual advantage and provided it
does not cause confusion to others present).

The division of the body of Christ into many churches,
communions and factions is the result of human sinfulness
and we are all called to repentance and conversion. We also
heed the urgent call of the Holy Spirit to give ourselves to
his work of reunion. But such a goal can be brought about
only by God's grace, not by human plans alone. We have to
avoid the temptation to abuse the Eucharist by opening it to
all Christians as though there was no disunity in the
Church. Instead the Holy Spirit calls us to bear the cross of
this division in the pain of not sharing a common table and
humbly to ask God's mercy on our petition to be one.

18 Given that the Catholic Church places such importance on marriage, why are Catholic priests not allowed to marry?

There are many misunderstandings today about priestly celibacy in the Catholic Church, probably because it goes so much against the grain of a society that is obsessed with sex.

The first of these is historical: celibacy, it is implied, was arbitrarily imposed on priests somewhere around the 12th century, one of those medieval practices which have nothing to do with the essence of the Gospel, let alone communicating it in today's world.

In fact, there is a long evolution behind the Church's discipline on celibacy for her priests. While it is true that St Peter, and possibly others of the apostles, were married, we must also remember that, in Peter's own words, they had "left everything and followed Jesus" (*Mt* 19:27). The implication is clear that those who had them had left their wives and families behind to become disciples.

This does not imply that all of them, or indeed all clergy in the first few centuries of the Church, were unmarried:

many priests, bishops and even popes had families. What
the documents of the Church from the 4th century on insist
on is that once ordained, a married man must cease to have
a sexual relationship with his wife. Furthermore, they
imply that this is not a new teaching, but one long
established as Church custom. (Given the scantiness of
records for the first two or three centuries of Church life, it
is not surprising that the first documents we have relating
to this date only from this time).

For most of the first millennium, very possibly from
the time of the apostles themselves, it was thus the
custom for married priests in the Western Church to live
apart from their wives after ordination. In the Eastern
Church a different discipline emerged, whereby at
ordination a man had to choose between marriage and
monastic life. Only monks could go on to become
bishops. What both Churches had in common was a strict
prohibition on marriage after ordination.

It can easily be seen that the Western practice of
married priests living 'as brother and sister' could lead to
many misunderstandings and problems. Thus when the
Second Lateran Council imposed celibacy on the clergy
in 1139, this did not come out of the blue, but was the
logical conclusion of a long process. Since that time,
celibacy has been obligatory for clergy in the Catholic
Church, though the Uniate church, which is part of the
Catholic Church while observing eastern liturgical and

canonical practices, has married priests, and exceptions can also be made for those who contracted marriage while clergy of another Church, such as the Anglican church, and who become Catholic priests.

The second misunderstanding is that obligatory priestly celibacy is based on a rejection of sexuality. It is true that some of the writings on this matter in earlier periods use language that we would not be comfortable with nowadays, implying that sexual intercourse renders a man unfit, or less worthy, to celebrate the Eucharist. It must be remembered that understanding of sexuality, and its place within marriage, has developed over the centuries, and especially in recent years with the insights of psychoanalysis and a more nuanced theology of married love. It would be unreasonable to expect earlier documents to reflect such insights.

The very fact that a different discipline is allowed for Uniate clergy and those who married in another church demonstrates that the Church does not consider married sexual intercourse a barrier to celebrating the Eucharist. The sexual aspect of celibacy must therefore be considered in strict relationship to its value as a sign of God's love which we look at below.

The final misunderstanding is that the discipline of celibacy is largely a practical matter of avoiding the tensions inherent in trying to combine priesthood with marriage and the raising of the family. While it is true that such practical considerations are by no means negligible, and that clergy, their spouses, and their children in other churches do sometimes suffer severely, there are also considerations to the contrary. Clergy can benefit from the support that a happy marriage brings, and their pastoral ministry may be enriched by the experience of family life. Practical considerations alone cannot be the basis for celibacy.

What, then, is the thinking behind this discipline? Fundamental to both Old and New Testament ideas about God's relationship with his people is the idea of a covenant, and specifically the covenant entered into at marriage. In Paul's letter to the Ephesians (5:25-32) the spousal love of Christ for his Church is explicitly related to his priestly offering of himself for her sanctification: "Husbands, love your wives as Christ loved the Church and gave himself up for her." The celibacy of the clergy is therefore not fundamentally something negative, but a sacramental sign of this exclusive love of Christ for his Church.

Celibacy is also a sign that there are other ways of exercising fatherhood than through physical generation, ways that are actually more important since they beget eternal life. The most obvious way this happens in the priest's ministry is through the sacraments, especially baptism, but it also takes place through preaching, teaching and spiritual guidance, which by the grace of the Holy Spirit can bring the life of Christ to birth and maturity in a person.

Such spiritual paternity is also a witness to the resurrection. Where there is no belief in the resurrection, physical paternity is obviously the only way for a man to realise a certain form of immortality or at least a continuance of life. Belief in the resurrection frees a person from that obligation, and celibacy therefore bears witness to the liberating newness of the Gospel, with its promise of eternal life.

Finally, in concrete terms, celibacy can be seen as a powerful way of imitating Jesus himself in his total self-giving to the Father and to the world. It is above all a witness of love from an undivided heart, and it is in this context that sexual renunciation must be seen, not in any sense of devaluing of sexual self-giving in marriage, which has its own generosity, discipline and fruitfulness.

19 Why dialogue with other religions if we believe there is only one God? Can those who are not baptised be saved?

The purpose of all dialogue is to understand oneself and others in the context of how we relate to and live with each other. Contemporary Britain is increasingly multicultural. The tragic events of 11th September and subsequent destructive acts put the place of religion in the modern world at the forefront. As a people in search of the truth we recognise the need to live in peace and harmony. This comes from better understanding the religious beliefs and practices of our neighbour.

Commencing with the documents of the Second Vatican Council, the Catholic Church has a rich treasury of teaching on the value of dialogue with other faiths: a teaching that affirms religious freedom by respecting human dignity.

The Declaration on the Relationship of the Church to Non-Christian Religions (*Nostra Aetate*) gives primary attention to what unites all people and what people have in common. We form one human family, with its origin in

God, and religion inspires a better understanding of the mystery, beauty and meaning of life. In the different religions of the world people search for inner peace, a quest manifested in teachings, rules of life and sacred rites. The Church does not reject anything that is true and holy in other religions, but rather looks upon them with sincere respect. Although different to our way of life and doctrine, the practice of others reflects a common search for truth.

How do we realise the search for truth? Pope Paul VI's encyclical on the Church (*Ecclesiam Suam*) challenges us to consider our relationship with God as a dialogue of salvation, a dialogue that begins as God's initiative and awaits a response without co-ercion. This call to dialogue is made through the ultimate expression of love: 'For God so loved the world that he gave his only Son' (*Jn* 3:16). The process of dialogue is a gradual one. As the path to holiness becomes clearer we discover that different ways lead to God. Dialogue not only enables us to understand difference better but to learn from it.

Pope John Paul II continued the prophetic teaching of Second Vatican Council, recognising the spiritual merits of other religions, heralding the need for dialogue and leading by example in meeting with leaders of various world religions.

Expressing his respect for religious liberty Pope John Paul II directed the following to the people of India: "I take this occasion to express my sincere interest in all the religions of India – an interest marked by genuine respect, by attention to what we have in common, by a desire to promote interreligious dialogue and fruitful collaboration between people of different faiths. In this regard, I note with admiration how the Indian constitution through its official recognition of religious liberty, honours the dignity of each person in his or her most sacred dimension, and at the same time allows the promotion of genuine spiritual values, which are so fundamental for social living" (New Delhi, 1st February, 1986).

Pope Benedict is committed to dialogue for a deeper understanding of the world's religions and of the common humanity that we share. At the inauguration of his pontificate, he affirmed that: "the Church wants to continue building bridges of friendship with the followers of all religions, in order to seek the true good of every person and society as a whole" (Address to the delegates of other churches and ecclesial communities and of other religious traditions, 25th April 2005).

The Pontifical Council for Interreligious Dialogue encourages dialogue at a local level. Greetings are issued at times of major festivals with the request that they be extended by the local Church.

The Church proclaims Christ as 'the way, the truth and the life' and calls for prudence and love in dialogue with others. Can those who are not baptised be saved? Yes.

While the word of God and saving power of Jesus Christ are enshrined in the Church, salvation in Christ is offered to all men and women. How this is effected in the case of those outside the Church is known to God alone. Clearly salvation is possible only for those who follow their conscience in leading a good life, but above all who respond to the grace of Christ which is offered to all. In no way, however, does this diminish the Church's responsibility to proclaim Christ to all as the only Saviour and Lord of humanity.

20 Why does the Catholic Church say so little about the environment?

As spiritual beings, we necessarily become aware of the spiritual dimensions of our environment. Nevertheless, we must be aware that environmental issues also have a moral dimension, and as such are connected to issues of justice. In his address *The Ecological Crisis*, Pope John Paul II acknowledged that now, 'faced with the widespread destruction of the environment, people everywhere are coming to understand that we cannot continue to use the good of the earth as we have in the past.' (*The Ecological Crisis: A Common Responsibility*)

At its most fundamental level, the environment is an ethical issue. The Church has a treasury of teaching on social justice. We are God's creation and our dignity is of paramount importance. Although the Church has recently begun to speak out on issues such as climate change and use of energy-producing resources, a deep concern for the created world is an integral part of the Church's view of a balanced human condition.

The positive dimension of this crisis is that humankind is coming to a greater awareness of the need for a harmonious relationship with the rest of creation. In his message for the world day of peace, Benedict XVI stated that 'disregard for the environment always harms human coexistence and vice versa'. A harmonious relationship with the created world is essential for human beings to realise what the Holy Father refers to as an 'ecology of peace.' (*Message for the World day of Peace*)

In this way, the Church views a harmonious relationship with the environment as an integral part of Christian anthropology. In his encyclical, *Pacem in Terris*, John XXIII addressed issues of interdependence. Human beings can only develop their full potential as children and heirs of God through cultivating a harmonious relationship with the created world. St Paul speaks of a 'new creation' (*Col* 2:18) which will renew the earth. In the same way, saints and theologians have spoken of harmony with the earth as an essential part of the spiritual path. In his *Canticle of the Creatures*, St Francis of Assisi describes God being praised through all creation. In his *Itinerarium mentis in Deum*, his later follower St Bonaventure details a path of spiritual ascent which begins with making peace with the created world.

A spirituality of creation is not new. The book of Genesis tells us that the earth is a gift 'to all living beings; all mortal creatures that are on the earth' (*Gn* 9:16-17) and that human beings are obliged to 'cultivate [the earth] and care for it' (*Gn* 2:15). In a manner consistent with the command that Jews observe the Sabbath, this care for creation should reflect the love of God.

Benedict XVI states that 'the mastery of man over Creation must not be despotic or senseless. Man must safeguard God's creation.' In order that this be carried out, the Catechism of the Catholic Church teaches: "The seventh commandment enjoins respect for the integrity of creation. Animals, like plants and inanimate beings, are by nature destined for the common good of the past, present and future humanity. Use of mineral, vegetable and animal resources of the universe cannot be divorced from respect for moral imperatives. Human dominion over inanimate and other living beings granted by the creator is not absolute; it is limited by a concern for the quality of life of one's neighbour, including generations to come; it requires respect for the integrity of creation." (2415)

Similarly, the Catechism of the Catholic Church reminds us of kindness shown to animals: "Animals are God's creatures. He surrounds them with providential care. By their mere existence they bless him and give him glory. Thus humans owe them kindness. We recall the gentleness of saints like Francis of Assisi or St Philip Neri." (2416)

By observing our teachings on the environment, we preserve what John Paul II referred to as 'the authentic conditions for a moral human ecology' (*Centesimus*

Annus). In the modern world, the Church has taken its role with regards to the environment seriously. Individual bishops' conferences have been given responsibility for the environment. In this way, the Church's response to the environmental crisis can be both immediate and relevant to the particular needs of each location. Through planting trees to offset its use of electricity, the Vatican has become the world's first carbon-neutral state. Similarly, parts of the Vatican are powered entirely by solar panels.

Benedict XVI writes, 'The destruction of the environment, its improper or selfish use and the violent hoarding of earth's resources causes grievances, conflicts and wars precisely because they are the consequences of an inhumane concept of development' (*Message for World Day of Peace*). The Church teaches that by achieving peace both with and in our world we can reach our human potential and live as God intended.

21 Isn't the Catholic Church's practice of nullifying supposedly invalid marriages divorce by another name?

The Catholic Church is often accused of dishonesty, if not cynicism, in claiming, on the one hand, that marriage is indissoluble while, on the other hand, offering to some people the possibility of a second marriage via the nullity procedure. The way to show how annulment and divorce differ is to consider the nature of marriage and the role of the law, both civil and ecclesiastical, in articulating and protecting the reality of marriage.

The Catholic Church teaches that marriage is "a covenant by which a man and a woman establish between themselves a partnership of the whole of life, by its very nature ordered toward the good of the spouses and the procreation and education of offspring; this covenant between baptised persons has been raised by Christ to the dignity of a sacrament." (*Catechism* 1601; Code 1055.1)

The first property of this covenant that the Church emphasises is its indissolubility: "This bond, which results from the free human act of the spouses and their consummation of the marriage, is a reality, henceforth irrevocable, and gives rise to a covenant guaranteed by God's fidelity. The Church does not have the power to contravene this disposition of divine wisdom." (1640)

In order to enter validly into this marriage covenant, a man and a woman must be free to marry, must exchange proper and free consent and must, if one or both of them are Catholic, do so according to the form prescribed by the Church, that is, canonical form. The absence of any of these essential requirements renders the marriage invalid and null. Nullity procedures are extensive and thorough because it is required that actual proof or at least moral certainty is obtained. The presumption, in other words, is always in favour of the validity of the marriage in question.

What would make a person not free to marry? Some things apply to everybody, because they affect the natural reality of marriage; others apply only to Catholics, because they affect the sacramental reality of marriage. About the former the Church cannot do anything; from the latter kind of impediments she can, for a just cause, dispense. The two in the former category are the existence of a previous bond of marriage; and impotence that is antecedent and perpetual. Sterility doesn't affect validity.

All other impediments, with the exception of some concerning consanguinity and affinity, are of an ecclesiastical nature and so bind only Catholics and those wishing to marry a Catholic and these can be dispensed.

So you have to be a minimum required age; there has to be a dispensation when a Catholic marries an unbaptised person; and an attempted marriage that involves a priest, or anybody vowed to celibacy is invalid. And you need a dispensation if you want to marry your first cousin.

So the Church could declare a marriage null if it was entered into invalidly on account of the presence of any of these impediments without dispensation. The more usual grounds for nullity are based on the absence of positive conditions necessary for validity. The crucial conditions concern consent: the exchange of consent must be free, and the parties must have the capacity, the knowledge and the will. The marriage is null if there is a defect in any of these conditions.

So if someone was pressured into marriage or married in order to escape the parental home, or on the rebound from a previous relationship, or under the influence of alcohol or drugs, or because he or she was too young and immature to make a life-long commitment, the tribunal may find sufficient evidence to prove that such a person was gravely lacking in the judgement required to enter marriage. Sometimes, the grounds will be of a strictly psychological nature, concerning factors that impede the free exchange of consent.

There are some obvious and clear justifications of nullity with which nobody would disagree. For instance, a marriage would be invalid if one of the parties deceived the other into thinking something about them which was untrue. This would be any matter about which one of the parties could honestly say: "If I'd known that I'd never have married him or her." Again, if you married the wrong person by mistake – someone's twin sister, for instance – it would be invalid. A marriage would also be invalid if it were entered into simply to obtain a visa or social security. But also, a marriage would be invalid if someone did not commit themselves exclusively to this one person: if, for instance, they intended to continue in another relationship incompatible with the marriage. It would invalidate a marriage if one of the parties intended to be unfaithful or with the intention that the marriage could end in divorce if it didn't work out.

In all these cases, the consent would be defective and the marriage therefore invalid and it would be for the marriage tribunal to prove that one or both of the parties entered the marriage with such an act of the will.

Lastly a marriage would be invalid if one or both of the parties intended permanently to exclude the possibility of children. This would be contrary to and incompatible with nature of marriage. It does not mean, however, that someone who is infertile, for whatever reason, cannot marry. It is the intention to exclude the possible that invalidates.

So, far from being divorce by another name, marriage annulment in the Catholic Church rests on the conviction that marriage has a definite and specific nature, that it is a serious business, requiring certain essential conditions and dispositions. Far from detracting from the serious nature of marriage, the marriage tribunals exist because marriage is too important to be taken for granted and cannot be lightly entered into.

22 Does the Catholic Church really teach that we are saved through good works, not faith?

The simple answer is that Catholics believe we are saved by faith in Christ, not by anything we can do by ourselves, but that to be authentic this faith must find expression in good works.

It is the clear teaching of Scripture and the Church that sin has caused a rupture in our relationship with God, and seriously damaged our ability to fulfil the destiny for which we were made, to live in communion with God. "All have sinned and fall short of the glory of God," says St Paul in his letter to the Romans (3:23). The results of this include moral chaos in our personal life, disharmony and strife in society, sickness and death.

We are not capable of putting this situation right by ourselves. It would be the height of presumption to suppose that we could somehow 'make God an offer' which would measure up to his infinite glory. In any case, since the very integrity of our will and intention has been compromised by sin, any move we made towards God would in itself be flawed. God himself, if he so chooses, must clearly take the initiative in restoring us to his friendship.

On the other hand, for God to do this without in some way involving us would undermine that dignity and freedom of choice which is precisely what has been so damaged in us. It would be paternalism rather than true love, and would not be able to arouse within us that freely given response in which true love consists.

For this reason, God in his infinite wisdom chose to redeem us by becoming one of us. In this way human nature itself, though it could not save humanity on its own, by being united to God in the person of Christ, was intimately involved in the salvation of humanity. The human nature of Jesus is a recreation of humanity to such an extent that he is called by St Paul the second Adam (1 *Co* 15:45).

In this sense salvation begins with the Incarnation itself, but is only completed by the perfect sacrifice of Christ on the Cross. Only the second person of the Trinity could offer to his Father a perfect act of loving atonement for our sins. Only a human being could offer that in an exemplary way by being lifted up on a Cross to suffer and die, and then rise again after three days. Thus the pattern is already established by which God alone can redeem us, but he chooses to involve our human nature in that process. This will continue in the way we participate in that salvation, and activate it, so to speak, in our lives.

This activation process is built on faith, which is itself a gift of God enabling us to recognise what Christ has done for us, and accept him as our Saviour and Lord. Since we cannot save ourselves, faith in what Christ has done for us is the indispensable point of entry into God's kingdom. When asked what doing God's work entails, Jesus replied, "This is the work of God, that you believe in him whom he has sent." (*Jn* 6: 29)

Such faith is an interior "work" in the human heart, but it must find expression in outward ways, by public profession, renunciation of evil and seeking baptism. Furthermore, many passages in the New Testament testify that "faith by itself, if it has no works, is dead" (*Jm* 2:17). It is not that good works save us by themselves, but they are a necessary part of that dynamism whereby human beings express in that outer lives what lies hidden in their hearts.

Only God can see the human heart and judge its deepest choices, but, as Jesus himself said, "A sound tree bears good fruit, but the bad tree bears evil fruit" (*Mt* 7:17). If our faith in Christ is accompanied, as it must be, by a real love for him, it is inconceivable that we would not want to keep the commandments he gave us and live the same kind of life as he did, in so far as we are able by God's grace. Otherwise the genuineness of our faith is called into question.

Faith is something dynamic and alive: it either grows or withers away. Faith is tested by the trials of daily life, and this is part of God's plan whereby he enables us to share in the working out of our own salvation, even though we are incapable of achieving it by ourselves. If by God's grace we respond to these challenges by good actions, our life in Christ grows stronger. If we retreat into ourselves or implicitly deny Christ by our actions, we risk losing the gift of faith itself. Our freedom to choose is an essential part of that dignity with which God created us and which he restores in Christ.

23 Isn't the doctrine of the Trinity at best a mathematical conundrum and at worst a plain contradiction in terms?

The Trinity is the central mystery of the Christian faith, the mystery from which all the doctrines of faith derive and to which they point. It is the central doctrine of Christianity that God is love, but the Trinity is known to us only because it is revealed to us: which is, of course, true of all love.

God is infinite, we are finite. He is a mystery, unfathomable and permanently beyond the reach of our minds. That God is a mystery does not mean, however, that we cannot know anything at all about him. But it does mean that we can never know or understand what it takes to be God: we cannot know, in other words, his nature or essence. But, at the same time, to say that God is a mystery, does not mean that we cannot say anything true about him. Rather, it means that whatever we can and do say about God is exceeded by God himself.

To speak of God as a Trinity does not lessen, but deepens, the mystery of God: our words become even more inadequate. But in speaking of the Trinity, we come to see that the distance between God and us is nevertheless bridged: not by knowledge, but by love - his for us and ours for him. And we come to see that our love for him is a sharing in the love that Father, Son and Holy Spirit – the Trinity – have for one another.

The doctrine of the Trinity is revealed to us by God himself; but it did not drop from the sky and nor was it culled ready-made from the New Testament. Nor is it a completed theory about God, answering all questions about God or, much less, explaining how the divinity works. The doctrine of the Trinity emerged in the course of the Church's effort to appropriate this revelation, this self-disclosure of God, as a coherent whole.

Technical terms were employed, but even these officially sanctioned formulations are inevitably inadequate to the impossible task of explaining how it can be that God is both three and one. It is beyond our comprehension. But the formulations are still vital because, under the guidance of the Holy Spirit, they guard Christian thinking from errors of various kinds and point us in the direction of the God we can never fully comprehend or know, except in love.

The doctrine of the Trinity was, of course, "a stumbling block to Jews and to the Greeks foolishness," but it is a belief rooted in the Jewish monotheism out of which Christianity arose, and it found expression in the philosophically sophisticated concepts of the Greco-Roman culture into which Christianity came.

Reflecting on their knowledge of Jesus and their experience of faith, Christians arrived at the conviction that their understanding that Jesus is God would be incomplete without recognising that what makes the life of faith possible, is the presence among us of the Spirit promised by our Lord. "No one", says St Paul, "can say: 'Jesus is Lord', except by the Holy Spirit."

But what exactly is the doctrine of the Trinity and what does it entail for our lives now? The teaching, put simply, is that there is only one God and that this God reveals himself and is known to us as Father, Son and Holy Spirit: three persons, each distinct and yet each entirely God. God, in other words, is a unity of substance and a diversity of persons. Their life within the single Godhead is one of total love and self-giving. And it is into this divine friendship that we are drawn through faith and baptism.

The doctrine of the Trinity is as an explanation of the assertion that God is Love, "the love that moves the sun and the other stars," as the poet Dante says. The doctrine of the Trinity spells out what it would mean to say that love is the deepest and most basic reality of all.

Jesus is God and, we believe, God is love. God, therefore, in some sense demanded by the nature of love, is a relationship. The Trinity is love given, love received, and loved shared. And the Christian life is a sharing, made possible by sanctifying grace, in this divine love.

We are made in the image and likeness of God, and this means that we are made in the image and likeness of the Trinity.

So the doctrine of the Trinity is foundational not only for our understanding of God but for our understanding of ourselves. This is God's own self-disclosure and it has only one purpose: to invite us to share in his life, the divine love which is the Blessed Trinity.

The mystery of the Most Holy Trinity is the central mystery of Christian faith and life. It is the mystery of God in himself. It is therefore the source of all other mysteries of faith, the light that enlightens them. It is the most fundamental and essential teaching in the 'hierarchy of the truths of faith'. The whole history of salvation is identical with the way and the means by which the one true God, Father, Son and Holy Spirit, reveals himself to us 'and reconciles and unites with himself those who turn away from sin'. (CCC 234)

24 Why does the Catholic Church refuse to ordain women as priests or bishops?

It is often complained that the Catholic Church is authoritarian and dictatorial in exercise of power. But the question of ordaining or not ordaining women has led the Church to declare that it lacks the authority to ordain women. This is neither a recent nor an eccentric position adopted by the Catholic Church: on the contrary, the ordination of women is an innovation on the part of a relatively recently formed division within Christendom and a departure from the constant tradition of both Eastern and Western Christianity.

In declaring that it does not possess the authority to ordain women, the Catholic Church is convinced that it is being faithful to what she has received from Christ. The sacraments, of which Holy Orders or the priesthood is one, are not the result of ecclesiastical or human invention, but given to the Church by Christ himself. The Church regards the sacraments as part of what is called the 'deposit' of faith, that which was given to the Church by Christ and handed down by the authority of the apostles through the generations. The sacraments are gifts the church has received and must guard.

Ordination is reserved to men because the Church is bound to follow what Christ himself did: he chose only men as apostles. This raises a fundamental point: the Church's existence is rooted in actual historical events, played out in contingent, historical circumstances rooted in time. Christ is an actual human being: this is the whole point of the Incarnation. His death is recalled as having taken place at a particular moment in history, in definite, specifiable circumstances: hence the mention in the creed of an insignificant, minor Roman provincial official, Pontius Pilate. The Church therefore cannot escape or circumvent certain historical facts: she cannot re-invent herself or re-fashion the heart of her belief in order to keep in step with the times. The Church cannot determine the recipients of priestly ordination in a manner that contradicts the actions of Christ himself, its originator.

It is often said that the ordination of men only reflects contingent, cultural circumstances that are, over time, open to change. But the fact is that Christ often demonstrated freedom from the cultural and religious conventions of his time. And even when he chose publicly to observe them, it was in order to bring them to fulfilment or to reveal their true purpose, not to accommodate himself to them. There seems no good reason to suppose, therefore, that his choice of men only was a cultural accommodation.

Again, it is often said that it is unjust to refuse women ordination. But here there is often confusion. Justice is the moral virtue that accords what is due to both God and neighbour. These days, justice and giving what is due are often understood solely in terms of equality – equal rights, equal protection under the law and, indeed, this same equality of dignity is a facet of the Church's life: all the baptised are equal in dignity, equally called to communion with God, and equally called to holiness and fullness of life in Christ. The question of justice in connection with the Church's teaching that it cannot ordain women arises only if you think that all the baptised have a right to be ordained. But, clearly, there is no such right, neither civic not spiritual. One's place in society is not inhibited by not being a priest and not being ordained clearly does not in any way contradict or constitute an obstacle to holiness, or fullness of life in Christ and communion with God. Ordination, in other words, is not necessary for salvation.

Significantly, the priesthood in discussions concerning the ordination of women is frequently considered in terms of 'leadership' and 'power'; the Church's inability to ordain women, it is alleged, excludes them from leadership roles and influence in the Church. The danger in this discussion is its narrow focus on only one aspect of the priestly role, and that not its most important aspect. A priest shares with all the baptised a role which our Lord

makes clear in the gospels should characterise all
Christians: it is his own role as a servant. We are all to be,
like him, servants, feet-washers, ministering to one
another. We are to be servants of one another, doing
without calculation or safeguards to our dignity, that
which is needed. This is to render the service Christ has
rendered us; this is the priesthood of all believers, in
which all the baptised participate.

And, within the priesthood of all believers, there is
another kind of specific service, which is a continuation
of that service rendered by the apostles, who were chosen
by Christ himself. This service, too, does not carry status
in any worldly sense and it is both a mistake to think it
does and a deformation of the role to seek it. It is a role
that originates in the choice made by our Lord of specific
individuals to carry on a particular kind of service in the
Church. All those specific individuals were, like Jesus
himself, men.

25 Could I be welcomed into the Catholic Church as a divorced person?

Everyone is welcome in the Catholic Church, and the Church, like Jesus her Lord, has a special care for those burdened with difficulties, whether of their own making or somebody else's.

God always takes us as we are right now, so whatever may have happened in the past, there is always the possibility of forgiveness, healing and putting things right. This includes especially the mistakes we or others have made in our closest relationships. The Church has a variety of ways of helping divorced people experience healing and a new start in their lives.

Part of the healing process is to recognise what we have done wrong in the past, not so as to perpetuate a sense of guilt, but to take responsibility and move forward in God's light and by his grace. In the case of divorce, this means some people will have to accept that they were partly or even largely to blame for what went wrong, while others may justly feel themselves to be an innocent victim.

In general the Catholic Church considers divorce to be seriously wrong, as it aims to break the indissoluble contract between husband and wife. However, we realise that at times it may be the only practical way forward, in which case it is not in itself a sin. This does not mean that the Catholic Church 'recognises' divorce, since until proven otherwise, we regard the marriage as still being in force. This is not an invention of the Church to make life hard, but is based on Our Lord's own teaching: "What God has joined together, let no man put asunder." (*Mt* 19:6)

A divorced person who has not remarried may become a Catholic and receive the sacraments. However they should be aware that they would not normally be able to remarry should they wish to do so in the future. Before remarrying they would need to apply for an annulment of their first marriage.

Catholics who are divorced and remarried are not able to receive the sacraments, but they still participate in the life of the Church in various ways, by attending Mass, listening to God's word, praying and taking part in the activities of the parish. They are full members of the Church.

This is not a judgment on their inner state of soul, which only God can see, but a consequence of the fact that externally their situation contravenes the permanence with which the Creator endowed marriage, and which both Old and New Testaments see as a reflection of the unbreakable covenant between God and the human race. The way the sacraments of the Church are dispensed must reflect this irrevocable love of God.

A divorced and remarried person, baptised in another Christian Church, while always welcome in a Catholic Church, could not therefore actually become a Catholic under normal circumstances, since it would be absurd for them to be received into the Church and then told they could not receive the sacraments. The same would apply to someone married to a previously married and divorced person.

If such a person wants to become a Catholic, there are two options open to them. He or she could seek an annulment of their first marriage (or the first marriage of their spouse). This is a recognition by the Church, after investigation, that the first marriage was not valid (it does not affect its legality or the status of children). Alternatively, they could decide to live as brother and sister, that is, without a sexual relationship, in their current marriage.

If, however, the first marriage of the divorced person was to a Catholic, and was not celebrated in a Catholic Church, it will probably be quite easy to demonstrate that this first marriage was not valid, leaving the person free to have their second marriage recognised by the Church and thus to become a Catholic.

Also, if a person has never been baptised, there is a special process by which it may be possible for their first marriage to be declared null and void if they wish to be baptised.

All this may seem complicated, but it can be summed up as follows:

All are welcome in the Catholic Church, but a welcome does not automatically mean being able to receive the sacraments. Those who cannot receive the sacraments are still fully welcome to be in the Church and take part in its life and worship.

In its pastoral practice the Catholic Church desires both to show care to the individual and to uphold the sanctity of marriage.